A Dog's Life

Poems by Adam Scheffler

Copyright © 2016 by Jacar Press

All rights reserved. No part of this book may be reproduced in any form or by any means without the prior written permission of the Publisher, excepting brief quotations used in connection with reviews.

Cover & interior design: Daniel Krawiec

ISBN 978-0-936481-11-1

Library of Congress Control Number: 2016943152

Jacar Press
6617 Deerview Trail
Durham, NC 27712
www.jacarpress.com

"Art is art.
The life it asks of us is a dog's life."

– James Merrill, "The Victor Dog"

"Joyful, joyful, joyful,
as only dogs know how to be happy
with only the autonomy
of their shameless spirit."

– Pablo Neruda, "A Dog Has Died,"
trans. Alfred Yankauer

Contents

At Play

Woman and Dogs	2
Statement of Purpose	4
Partner	6
Two Short Poems About Joy	8
Walking Around: The Sixth Wave of Extinctions	9
Real Night	11
Sex Positive	12
Relationship Quiz	13
Americas	14
Carson Daly	15

Out for a Walk

Web	18
Get a Dog	20
Star-Nosed Mole	21
My Body	22
Ghazal	24
Old-Time Gizzards	26
1WTC	28
Soldiers at Night	30
Contemporaries	32
On the Discovery that Oleic Acid is the 'Dead Smell' Of Ants	34

Dog Days

Ocean	36
Great Grandfathers	37
A Nursing Home in Kentucky	38
Waitress	40
Ode to Katie's Hairy Armpits	41
Blind Date	42
At the Airport	43
Gym Guy	44
Un-Relatable Poem	45
The Car Accident	46
Obama's Oval Office	47

Baying at the Moon
My Robot   50
My Failed Poems   51
A Walk on the Beach   52
Anti-Acknowledgements   53
You are dead, Lewis Carroll   55
Ivy League Graduation Speech   56
Theme Park   57
The New Me   58

In the Fields
The Hair   60
No other world   63
Walmart Poem   64
Williamsburg, Kentucky   65
Love Poem for Lindsay in an Iowa Tornado Ten Years Ago   66
Leap Day Birthday   67
Every Dog Has His Day   68
I Have Lots of Hearts   69
My Other Grandparents   70
Birthday Poem   71

Acknowledgements   73

For Lindsay

At Play

Woman and Dogs

My girlfriend's dog is small and fat and neurotic
and smells at night like an African meat flower.
It loves her more than some people love anyone
in a riddle of love it worries at, lying there on the floor.
As she writes it makes strange sounds:
lickings, sighings, suckings, shiftings
like the worrying-tide of the world, like the vast
dog-tide of the world in its love of the moon
and of fetching sticks. My girlfriend is very quiet
and very white like the moon, and some people think
she is cold and uncaring just like it.
But her dog knows better, it knows she is quiet
like the sun as she writes her stories
tapping them quietly with her fingers, shaping
the messages she has heard of painful warmth
and love, quietly as a tree repeating the hard message
of the sun in its devotion of leaves and listening.
I have listened carefully to the dog. I have stolen
the dog's secret about her. I have figured it out.
She is quiet and so she writes long stories
and I am loud and so I write quick poems
tiring myself out more quickly to look up at her
as lovingly and neurotically as the dog
perhaps never as lovingly as the dog
who unlike me has nothing to prove
who does not write poems except the thought-poems
of the chase, the sky, the walk, the meal.
Sick of the dog, I have had too much also of poems
petulant, filled with strange achings
I think of my navel which is too deep like a mine

I send my finger into it like a canary and feel sad
and weird and know I will die. But sometimes
she tells me she likes my chest and I take her
in my arms and feel for once superior to the dog.
Before this dog she had another dog I never met, a
golden retriever, who was not at all neurotic
who swallowed her childhood happily
like a white spiral fossil and brought it back
covered with a fine varnish fine slobber of evening
and died, and now is only a picture in a cheap frame
on the top of her desk as she writes. It makes me think
of all I can't see: the long list of books she gave me
how they existed all my life and before it
and her story right now invisible to her too
like the idea of a flower to all the roots underneath
their gossipy brags and worries: how their flowers
grow tall as the spine of a young boy, go blue
as a nun's lips in winter, unless the earth goes
upwards forever unbroken – but there she is
at least, complete: watched by the dog who is dead
watched by the dog who smells bad and is alive
watched by me, who am sick of poems and of life too maybe
but am alive and glad to look at her, at the tiny mark
on her cheek where the clamp brought her forth kicking
from the womb to sit one day quietly in the
wound and fury of writing before the three of us
who cannot help, who wait in aches and shiftings
for her to turn round and speak gently our names.

Statement of Purpose

The lamppost believes in the transmigration of souls,
the sweater-vest only believes in lambs
and the window in burning things alive.
My neighbor believes in the constitution of the United States tonight
affixing his guns like books to the walls of his bedroom.
I've never fired a gun but I believe in recoil, though
the monster in my closet doesn't believe in me any longer
despairing, itching his scaly chest.
On Telegraph Avenue in Berkeley the prophet believes
in Che Guevara t-shirts and eating ramen noodles
which believe they are brains sometimes
when someone wearing a blindfold touches them.
If everyone suddenly started believing in death
the TV would shut down and the soldiers would drop it
too ashamed of what their moms would think, and of wetting their beds.
If I started believing in death I'd find Marlene again,
I'd take another crack at philosophy.
Wet noodles also feel wonderful anytime, taboo.
A man with an arrow in his head is rector of my church
where the janitor has an arrow in his heart
and sings beautifully when no one is listening,
prying the gum like wacko toadstools from the backs of the pews.
Did the dinosaurs admire sunsets, do animals
like them, did Neanderthals, does Hallmark,
do you just want it to be over quickly?
Sometimes a weirdo on a double decker bike shoots through
the noon path of my life, naked, with blasé that could kill stones.
Sometimes I want to spit on flowers.
I love when the interrogator, the torturer, confesses her love
for her prisoner, it is never a lie, as even the elevators rising

and falling tonight believe in innocence,
as the cops believe in justice and themselves.
As the snow falling believes in calmness deep in the
grain of things, making stairs into impossible pristine
lumps winding up the building sides,
and today is a benchmark for the prisoner as he takes
another step down the plank, and says he'll go
farther tomorrow. He cries out, and the birds answer excitedly.
He doesn't believe it will ever end.

Partner

Since we're not married and
have been together so long
boyfriend and girlfriend is
starting to sound too hip, too sexy
for what we are, too Parisian –
like we take long strolls
on the Seine or make love in front
of mimes, like we tie our bodies
into balloon animals and float,
or ride the train under the
slimmest finger of ocean
to London, imagining Sherlock Holmes
hot on the trail of Moriarty
for the hundredth time too stupid
and obsessed to know his own
love for Watson if it hit him in the
face. They are partners, and I think it's
time for us to steal their appellation
of dusty trusty hue that they stole
from Western Marlboro men
chewing tobacco and spitting
on cactuses, and not pronouncing
the "t," as they moved
through the canyons, muscular
thighs draped over their horses.
We too journey side by side
on the trusty steeds of twin beds
or the single gigantic steed of a
California king, so my nighttime
imitations of a ninja won't bother you,

so your thin form can be rolled up
like a cigarette in blankets
and be smoked by night
and the long plume of your dreams
can stay private. I love
how it's all taken on faith,
the way day is partner to night,
or yesterday to today, knowing
no covenant keeps it all
together, no words stored
in a courthouse or promises made
before people who think love
is sealed by their getting drunk
for free, or by throwing rice on us
to plant in us a field we
we work all our lives –
I want you no sidekick or wife,
but choosing to be with me
and me with you day by day, stealthy
capable human partners planting
flags in a private happiness
without tiny sherpas of us
climbing to the top of a cake,
without the cake being sliced
into and floated out amidst a flock
of endless friends and relations
each jostling for the piece
with extra sugar – with the
frosting in which is written
congratulations and our names.

Two Short Poems About Joy

1. Porn

The worst thing about porn being
its prudery about
what the body mostly looks like,
its need to be touched and loved
even with tiny boobs or penises
the size of toothpicks,
even if above the age of 40,
or if the sex you want to have is so
boring and vanilla nobody
could watch it all the way through,
the moans almost inaudible
and all the same, the climax merely
a gripping of sheets like grass.

2. God Backwards is Dog

As if the opposite of God
was the dog tugging its way on its leash
in an arc so when you reel it in, it will grasp
the turd its been eyeing between
two clamped jaws. This is where 'shit
eating grin' comes from: which means
a happiness so great and not ours it's
irritating, the way conversation is
when it requires you to listen,
which dogs never do, because unlike God
they want to ask of us as little as possible,
or take only what gives us hope by their
taking – walks under the live oaks,
pettings, which I shall now think of
as inverse prayers to inverse Gods
who just want their butts scratched and
to do a little jig of thanks;
and who are you to think that's comical
for isn't the inverse of holy also holy,
and probably more so?

Walking Around: The Sixth Wave of Extinctions

Afternoon in February mild hangover after the decade no one knows
still how to name, and the sunlight spending itself
lavishly on the first elm leaves like nipples willing a body around them
and the birds won't shut up a hundred tiny nameless and yet
unconfused, as if entitled to this sunlight to rise and settle back in
wire, elm, wire. And right out the door children with green plastic
soldiers – they still make those – guarding the edges of
flowerpots which I guess are islands and the dirt is the sea.
And now by the shops the streetman has attached 30 strings to his body
which go rattling ornaments, bristling kinetic sculptures, pinwheels,
horns, stars, shaking and tingling. It is the end of winter, it is a kind
of sharpening, a glow that turns from pain's swizzled core, from the
sixth great wave of extinctions, man-made, right onto Brattle street
and the great mansions of the Tories Robert Lowell would once
write glumly of – to this good errand of buying Valentine chocolates as
a girl so beautiful walks by – and then one of the gloves hanging on
the wintry bush its cryptic commentary one encounters every so often
on all the blunders plugged into the variable of the earth. As for the sky
it is layered red-pink-blue like a science project as the old women
in front, scared by my brisk pace, look behind so I am the feared thing –
I knew it, a headline. How the woman tripped and fell into the Picasso
and reduced its value by half. To fall into a Picasso! Exactly how
yesterday at the museum the meteors were all getting named after the
places they crash into, and so yesterday became the Day of the Museum's
Extinct Snake Skeleton, its three hundred vertebrae like a spiral banister
in hell – which would really be better to see with the person you're
sleeping with – and for an instant now I feel as though every loved place
or good fact or right person is a mirror shard of the Garden and if

we could only gather them back – but already the sun like a
bright coin is going round and round the funnel of the sky into
its hole and collection drawer, and already the buildings and trees
are pure dark outline against a sky gone black to blue to palest seagreen
(Schuyler: "another day, sob, dies") (Leonardo: only spirals are both
active and passive!) and I am feeling alert and only a little neurotic as
the car motions me on past the tiny art gallery the size of a woodshed.
At home the keyhole is dark and I read how the last great auks, maybe
a mated pair, were clubbed to death in 1844, and how the Dawn Redwood
which was thought to be extinct two million years ago was found
alive in China for no other reason than sometimes things come back.

Real Night

I miss it – no streetlamps, where
you have to depend on the moon, where soccer
at dusk in an open field
is a void full of voices and shadows
ringing out, forming, scattering –
even this walk in Indiana, late June,
10 PM when we're outside the woods
we can still see them.
Notes from the electric guitar drift over
from the restaurant, half-mile distant
lit up like a deep sea fish.
Real night is going extinct, you
tell me, a sole astronomer has it
lives so high up in the Alps, in the starlab alone
that he says he never wants to come down
never wants to leave the stepping outside
from note-taking and instruments
into the conflagration, unshared, only *his*
silent stars, drunk with blackness?
I take your wrist to feel the thin bones.
The dog stays close for once brushing my leg.
There are still hints of real night
here, I think: fireflies scattering
constellations down open tunnels of trees,
beckoning *this way* – or the stag earlier,
standing at the dusk edge of the woods,
tearing at hanging leaves, glaring through
round black eyes, slipping
into the forest-hole behind him – or now,
entering those woods, the bullfrogs calling
and calling, drowning out the guitar in
their touch-swamp: gorgeous pure and empty,
branches streaming over our heads,
warm breeze on our faces on our cheeks.

Sex Positive

I'd like to be sex positive,
but I don't know what that means. Positive
as in all wanted sex is good – or positive
that I don't want to be a religious nut, sex negative?
Thing is, I think a willingness to see the negative
is necessary, and I don't trust pluck or positivity
when they are a policy. I'm policy negative
though obviously I want people to have a good positive
time with all their butt plugs and spankings, I'm positive
I do. Yet gloryholes, facials, etc. seem kind of negative –
to thrive on humiliation and degradation, on negative
fantasies of misogyny or power – negative
name calling – slut, whore, etc. – which doesn't seem too positive.
I understand – I think – the allure of negatives,
being overpowered, fucked, or mastering – negatives
are thrilling, hot, dangerous whereas positives
'lovemaking' 'sharing, respectful sex' can seem positively
boring, and less honest. Yet so much of that which I'm positive
I want, I've learned, has its negatives –
the desire to talk all the time and never listen, say is negative
as is the desire to eat tortured goose liver – pretty negative.
I know our brains get wired certain ways that we're positive
we can't change – and this isn't always that negative.
I definitely don't want to ban all negatives.
But maybe we can allow ourselves to see both positives *and* negatives
maybe we can allow ourselves to think that sex
is more complex a math than just arithmetic of positives and negatives
and talk more openly about what hot negatives
are simply leftover patriarchal bullshit negatives
and which can be sublimated to make fucking truly positive.

Relationship Quiz

It's your guy's birthday what are you getting him?

Only a kiss – like two leashed hummingbirds, a wild thrumming of faces.

You're out with a friend and spot a cute guy, you...?

Slowly sidestep the sloth of ego.

When talking with a cute guy, you...?

Give him five moments to say at least one interesting thing, otherwise burn your possible family and its complex misfortunes to ash.

What bra is your spirit animal?

The penguin bra, the dung beetle bra, the bra of twilight.

What celeb gets you?

Foreclosed playgrounds covered in rust.

What's your favorite part of sex?

If there have to be thoughts then let them spurt with surprise at your tigerish thighs, your back, the dry river of your hair.

You're going to a party what do you wear?

An entire bag of nectarines. No, the skin of the Maccabees.

The last time it didn't work out with a guy, what happened?

What was there I cannot say, and now I drift, half-dreaming, canyons and offices, soon lost to sight out a bus window.

What's your sexual fantasy?

When I cum, for passenger pigeons to be no longer extinct.

What's Your Dream Date?

To know that the part of me that stood at my uncle's deathbed cold, feeling nothing, will be dredged up at last like an old ship filled with slime.

Americas

O thank you, Lord, for modernity, now shoo:
you can have half of America,
the other half goes to the dog lovers.

The real America and the false America though are
getting along quite well recently. They are
meeting on the sly, they are having tea
and pretending to be British.
'Rarara I'm the Queen' say both Americas at once
grinning, holding out to each other
their prismed hands made of every ethnicity.

When a little America is born into the world
it is very perplexed and tries to make sure
nobody can have an abortion.
When it grows up, many wings sprout
from its back, and it talks to itself incessantly
about who shot who.

Carson Daly *(after Christopher Smart)*

For I will consider Carson Daly.
For in his youth he considered becoming a Catholic priest, but was too much of a sensualist.
For he is still known as the holy man of the industry and has a jacket embroidered that says so.
For he wants us to honor time's passage and encourages young singers with beautiful voices.
For he helped discover Alanis Morissette whose anger helped me in high school.
For if in high school I hated him now I am pleased whenever his face illumines a TV.
For the sun of Santa Monica has shined kindly upon him.
For he is over 40 and aging well despite 16 years in the business.
For his voice can be heard late at night and just before dawn on the radio like an albatross for the lonely.
For he loves suits but is known to sport a casual cap.
For he loves golf and nothing makes him happier than a well-manicured green field.
For a green field reminds him above all of neatness, which pleases him best.
For he proclaims that America is tired of catfights and viciousness.
For he has been described as vanilla, which is the most popular flavor.
For other flavors are merely gimmicks but vanilla endures.
For vanilla is the color of fresh snow and in Spanish means *little pod*.
For vanilla reminds him of his mother's milk which as a babe he drank greedily and with joy.

Out For A Walk

Web

The hermit Professor died in May and left
a dirty house, a helpless husband, and
5000 pages of her scribbled unread mathematics.
So now my father, 3000 miles away, has
to make sure that someone is making sense of them
in case there is a brilliant idea in there
somewhere, and they're all written in a private script
that will require decoding before deciphering,
and he has to arrange with social services
to help the husband, who hasn't talked to another
human being, except for his wife, in years,
learn how to drive and get groceries and
use the internet. My father has to do all this
because the hermit professor recruited him
to his first real job, and then for years my father was
the couple's only real friend, only one they would
invite to their house where the clocks were different
from the rest of the city, an hour off say,
no protection from the sun rising and setting.
No doubt, each life is a mess, and it doesn't help
anyone that I'm another to think this today
in July, looking up at a spider web, empty
and spread in patchy gap-tooth horizontals
where somehow a fly – one of those tiny white ones
that mist about the porch all morning like bits of ash
and live for only a week – has managed to die.
Yet I can't see the dead woman's house
and I can see this web – full of barren bits, wings, legs,
sticks and seeds, brittle and pointless and bending
in June light in pockets in wind over the stairs.

If my careful father were a spider
he would never have built this, he probably
would be living for another dozen seasons
with flies saved for winter and each piece of his webbing
spaced exactly one inch apart with perfect radial
spokes and backup ballast strands in case any of them
got knocked into. I'm not so careful,
I'm more like a stingy version of the dead professor
who gave me, for my Bar Mitzvah,
the largest gift of money I've ever received
from someone who wasn't my parent and who did it
– we had met only once – out of love for my father and belief
in his life and work. I will live a different life
from my father, and may make a greater mess of it
than his mentor professor, leave more
wreckage behind: but right now I feel happy,
feel free to bless my father and myself
in my own way: sitting on a porch,
not helping anyone, in my shorts and bare feet, fiddling
with poems, looking up at ragged patterns
stitched on air, stilted and turning half-invisible
in sunlight where the maker has disappeared,
and a tiny white mouth closes forever.

Get a Dog

It's good to see someone staring up at your nude body
without a sign of interest
and to have someone to share all your
vices with, giving a tithe of 10 percent of all snacks;
yes it widens and inflates the soul
to give regularly and not to feel braggy about it,
and to be allowed to bury a loved one in your
own backyard for once, beneath the outhouse of
their own favorite lemon tree –
even to see your yard riddled with curious holes the
gophers and snakes move into is healthy and
reminds you you don't really own anything –
and gives you an excuse to be outside alone
without getting lung cancer – or frightening the
neighbors by your wish to be introspective;
and who but dogs will teach you an appropriate
fear of small children, or how to perceive
the ghost-world of secret smells like **ESP**
– so no two fences can be passed without admiration –
or pull you into the chase like a nature show
where you can hold the tiger back at
the last second so everyone can go home,
but still allow it the joy of the hunt.

Star-Nosed Mole

I think my veins run into each other in a loop.
That's why I keep breaking vows,
jumping over hedges, baying at the moon.

I wonder if there's some consistency in
me more than being a Rube Goldberg machine
for death, and would I feel better if I knew
my life were at least kindling for a firefly's tiny star?

I want some follow through, to stop up my ears
to the siren songs of entertainment,
learn to backstroke in boredom, feeling
the meniscus kiss my ears and lie to me
about the immortality of my particles.

That we were all once part of stars is useless
information with a late night infomercial
hammering on about the first electric spatula.

I carry eight devils on my shoulder, weeping
and several angels who are so undercover
they've forgotten their names. I hunch
over examining earthworms in puddles in the rain.

I sing to my plants to make them shrivel,
or wander the lanes checking my email
over and over like a ripple seeking
a brook. Skipping down the street at

night, under the bellicose horned stars,
I have no warrants out against me,
I am fearless as a turnip awaiting the plow.

My Body

So far I have liked having a body.
Sometimes, throbbing with bite marks,
it fills with gurgles and omens.
In the dark, it pulses.
Blood runs through my body like a comb.
Sometimes I envy broken waves their
accomplished pang on the shore, one waveful
how much easier wave/water
than body/soul or body/heart/mind/soul
which is like being a broken cuckoo clock
filled with several stuck painted birds.
I wish others at least would see and appreciate
all the fingerprints staining my skin.
Some perks though: getting muddy, sweaty,
roughing it – making do, getting along.
I don't like that I have to eat things.
It is common sense to eat things
but I don't like it. It's not just "orders swallowed
broken down, transferred through membranes
to strengthen larger orders" like Ammons says.
It's meat and meat is wrong.
Although I don't mind shitting or farting
and I love how eyelids make such a difference.
I wonder if fish dream, and, if so,
what it's like always to dream with your eyes open –
if it's like having a stage in front of you
(reefs, grit) as your dreams file in
with their quicker electric bodies.
Suggestions for improvement: the same
but always naked, the same

but with torn out wings.
When we meet, we touch each others'
scapulae, carefully like after sex.
This way we go about naked, trembling
and very expensive. One day I know
I'll vomit out my birds, my body
will shrivel, and shitting
will be less pleasant.
I'll grow smaller to make room
for death to enclose me in its tight brown egg.
That's why it's so important after sex
to touch each other and listen to our organs,
how innocent and ugly they are, there, fluttering.
It's the only good time to think about anatomy –
as orgasms make room for childhood
to peek out in quick blue flutes of our blood.
Or if I move fast enough, down a slide,
or a roller coaster, I can feel two
versions of me overlapping in a Venn diagram
with a grin shared, whirled in the middle.
When I stop they become one circle
tingling in place as if strummed.
As if I could never tear myself on thorns
or have holes bored into me
because having a body means
being too slippery and new.

Ghazal

A blimp floats in the pink sadness of another one's country.
It's 2009, a Friday, and spring has come to my country.

Leo in Acco joins tonight's field of soccer.
Tomorrow night's game is Arab. It's a Jewish country.

1910: my great-grandfather, alone, peers out from the train.
Hills' green tribulation. Soon life in a new country.

Lindsay rereading Huck Finn near the Creation Museum
with its Christmas light dinosaurs. Oh my bruised country:

Which is sadder a burn hole or a moth hole?
Which is sadder to belong or not to belong to a country?

Ashbery says in my ear at 14 he loved coffee and Chopin.
I'm 25, headphones on a run. We live in the same country.

In daybed, the couple vibrates like dragonflies trying to catch.
A child draws the green border of a make believe country.

Amichai: her love cries name-out the birds.
Shakespeare guffaws at the pleasures of the country.

But then: what distances of water splashed up onto your face
to awake you, first morning of your visit to this country?

The stripper sways in Paris on high-heeled glass slippers.
We do not perform torture inside our country.

My grandfather shoots himself in the head. My mother
hears of this, how? In the cracks, lie hidden countries.

My childhood slobbers softly onto my arm. The Talmud:
save one life – you save the whole world – but no countries.

All day, our names sink and fester, like far, dim potatoes.
All night, the humans leak, throbbing, into the country.

American scientists free speeches in Sweden:
Karin says they remind us we *can* love your country.

That a pink hand should place its flag in true innocence
over the shoulders of a shivering country?

Old-Time Gizzards

I'll not give the world over to death
without a discussion first,
and when I lick stamps I feel like the sea.

I dance nakedly in my clothing wishing
I could be more discrete without lying
like a cyclone touching down in a bottle
thinking it's furious, but
sweetly touching as blue underpants.

To be more directly furious!
To be famous to animals –
stags bowing down their chandeliers
and the turkeys a gobbling paparazzi.

Or to speak with Obama in 30 years when
he has Alzheimer's and tell him over
and over each day, "you were president!"

Flowers keep dripping from my armpits
so I must hold my arm up, which is boring
but how else to get spring going again?

And the clouds have landed so our
very breath is gray and obscure.

Prove to me you're more alive than a fern.
Why would you want to be?
I leave you scattered notes like breadcrumbs
leading to a 50% off coupon
at the Black Friday of joyful distraction.

People poo-poo distraction as below their
dignity, which is about as much fun as the
plaster at the Statue of Liberty's feet

while meanwhile, each tree marries
spring and wears a veil of green
for a few months and then gets a divorce
and I try to slaughter as many sheep
as possible to sleep easy,

drifting out from myself in a boat made out of
optimistic stock projections.

1WTC

Sometimes I lie in bed at night
with the shade pulled back,
and count all the lights still on.
This morning, in the distance, it hoists a scaffold
of shouting workers high in the air
who struggle to latch and graft its glittering
spire into place, the one needed
to reach its symbolic 1776 feet.

I hate the simplicity of its most American message:
we can do anything –
knock us down, we'll rise up stronger –
and I think how little we've learned,
though it's not unbeautiful, its bent
glass-sheen and shimmer. 'At sunset
it takes on the color of the sky,' says the doorman.

From my room at night it can seem delicate,
distant, even small, but running south
along the Hudson it grows
so quickly that I feel quickly helpless:
I see the simple myth of innocence
and perseverance writ large
in its monstrousness and I tilt my head back
until I see black in the corners of my vision.

I try to see in it those many who won't
ride the elevators into the sky,
who won't vacuum the floors, or barter for stocks,

or else to glimpse in it the families
who watch the new tower rise
up better and higher, like an elaborate
eulogy telling only a person's best qualities,
one that in its very ethereal perfection teaches you
for the first time, that your beloved is dead.

Soldiers at Night

Wrapped in bed how can they sleep without
knowing they do so? Without feeling themselves
alone in their cots? – no bunks of soldiers around
them, just empty extension, room after room for their
hollowness, their small itching breaths, their minds
turned vast and spectral, looming – here is the tug
where the string in their minds (weighed down with
their days) drags them towards the other,
their other – secret lives mostly forgotten.
But tonight the pull is weak, tonight they fear sleep
as they fear death – like gods in the void unsure of
what to create. They picture a hill, grass, a path
on the hill splitting twice off to houses, but continuing
to where the hill ends in a cliff with the sea below it,
blue and infinite, the infinite causing the blue
or vice versa as the day dims and electric torches
blare into life – making the path all that is visible,
making it the visible world. They hold onto that path,
extend it. It blazes white as a lady's token, tattoo,
or girlfriend's lower back, untouched by the sun —
they extend it, they pull the path then over the hill,
the cliff, above the ocean and out, bringing daylight
everywhere back – blue daylight – and the path,
white as a flag rubbed clean of its symbols,
stretching out, becoming both runway and plane
in the daylight, blue daylight. And now they are inside
that plane, they are afraid of turbulence
but wanting a little, not for excitement, no, but for
a need not to lose, a need to *give up*. The boy
watches the airplane movie with no headphones

and everyone laughs – a joke he cannot hear –
but only he can see them in the dark rows of the plane,
only he can hear this laugh, and only he notices
this one moment when the hero leaps and everyone
stops breathing... and now the soldiers sleep
in their cots, dreaming of sleepers no longer on
planes and perhaps not even God can know
the moment they fell asleep, the moment that could
change the universe forever, imperceptibly, sleep:
the pure ritual, the ritual for rituals' sake.

Contemporaries

Every dog born at your birth is now dead
every bottlenose dolphin and beaver
every mallard and mountain lion.
In the first 30 minutes of your life
all the fruit flies your age were dead.
Death started small:
when you turned three the last ant
your age turned its six legs to heaven.
When you blew out your first candles
your fellow bee ladled itself gently
into a flower. Now in spring you
meet their great-great-great-
grandson in a rose or hyacinth.
In 4th grade, the last prairie dog peered out.
As you had your first sexual experience,
the last goat born on your birthday
rubbed its itchy head against
the fence, bleated, and expired.
In your 20s, death snuck past
the last porcupine's quills.
The cats and pigs like Virgil could only take you
half way through them too,
and turning 30 the long-faced
Beatrice of bison left you
as they left America, were hustled out
by drunk poachers firing bored
out of train windows, as all the tapirs
will go without your ever seeing one of them
(though they apparently live alone and have sex
in and out of water).

In your middle-years the last chimp
chucked his banana, the last Macaw
lost its luster, the last toad croaked,
and the last Asian elephant,
more fragile than the African versions, collapsed,
was buried in a spot the younger ones,
trunks swaying like chimes,
refused to step on as they tossed the sad, cooling
earth onto their backs.
At sixty the last eagle plummets.
At seventy, the parrot who repeated all your
phrases goes mute. Silence fills
the room. After we are gone
what will linger? A few swans
will spit on our graves and be hateful,
a few turkey buzzards
born in their season will pick
at the bones by the highway,
themselves soon crushed
and peeled back to feathers.
And then only the swimming
things will remember the 20th century,
the bowhead whale dodging harpoons,
the sea turtles playing in the
turquoise waves of Kauai, and almost
mindless in their dazzling pink
and white pack, the koi
who keep rising toward the
rippling surface of the lake
to take their food from another world.

On the Discovery that Oleic Acid is the 'Dead Smell' Of Ants
(for E.O. Wilson)

Bits of feces, extract of fishrot, and gymsweat
for weeks my lab smells like
"sewer, garbage dump and locker room,"
and cackling, yes I suddenly have it, moon-eyed
over the colony, let's see this go: paperclip
or pebble now 'Problems to be Solved'
schlepped to the deadpile, ziggurat of
ant-bones. Now I hold the dropper over
a single ant, now I let the single drop fall:

I am dead – I can smell it. I was a member
once of the Two Lines, I did its purpose,
and now they hoist and carry me, now they
fling my life, so much offal, into the rest –
we had been carrying leaf-bits
their slivers their task and now the death
smell cinches up all around, like water,
I am inside it. It is my new element, my
ceiling, my floor – but I can move,
can climb up through the bodies, wriggling
to limb-snap and shudder, their yield.
I can step and push off of a face, hug
a thorax, gasp to reach limbs through
to the air, to the Giant's eye, the ten moons,
the Floating Tunnels and fully pull out
my body from the crush and totem,
and their great stench is behind me, and
here death even runs off me a little. I taste it,
and it melts. I lick it from my body, take
its whole coat off with my tongue, and here
is my old life waiting underneath
like any casual dawn. And here are
the lines, and now I re-enter their tide,
am accepted into their singular purpose,
and death was a problem and I solved it.

Dog Days

Ocean

You can search me,
but I am all pockets
each the size of Poland.

I have more eco systems
than wet dreams,
more tuna and squid
than thoughts in your head.

For each dream you have
I offer you the salty oblivion
of morning.

For each numbskull who'd
plumb my depths, I offer
you another day,
a raven without a branch.

You can poison me:
my jellies collect like wildfire,
a continent – garbage blossoms
through me like acne,
plastic rings, condoms, trash bags.

These days, I take my offerings
where I can, these days
you visit at my corners unable
to see me; I am something
vast at the corner of your vision
studying you
without expression.

Great Grandfathers

They sit quiet in murmuring
restaurants, at family gatherings,
wearing old paisley ties and tweed,
hands folded on their laps,
ready to ask for the one thing
on the menu they can order
for old age means fewer choices.

At the end of the table
they float on pillows, counting out
the abacus of their pills
for they are unhearing
though their ears are swollen up
big as cabbages in lovely whorls,
cobwebs, funnels gathering darkness.

Their boredom is loud though,
a knot we try to untie with talk.
They catch a few words, maybe,
or let them drift past like feathers,
turning their eyes inwards
to the root cellar where memories
and dreams grow twined.

A Nursing Home in Kentucky

The parking lot lights shine
successively in on the taxidermized
white tiger and badger and puma

locked in their advanced positions
of fury, of formaldehyde
with marbles laid over their scooped

out eye-spaces, orbiting the bedstead
of the old hunter-man who moved into
this nursing home totally

healthy to make catcalls and
sob to the nurses about his love
for himself.

Here you must follow
a quarter mile of neon
signs to the egress

where the healthier old wander
back and forth along glass corridors
biting their nails

their various ailments contained
perfectly by bodies which are
themselves contained perfectly by the

building shaped to their wanderings
like the grains inside a rainstick
sliding forth, sliding back.

It is not really a home but
you will never leave this place where
you peer from the high

one-way mirror into an outside
where the pigeons and one
hefty bag line a telephone pole

and lean off into
a distance you cannot see
into, into which they fling

their raptor-bodies, tiny
but with such deft hunger
like a pro-unhooking all

the buttons from a cocktail waitress's
shirt, in a single musical gesture – like notes –
as evening unravels and spills

its stale, defunct beauty
over that empty lot, full of
tree shadows, and stains us with its orange

and pinks whose promise
of romance keeps everyone alive
and unfulfilled.

Waitress

Half the men in here tonight
are in love with her,
ordering twice as much wine
as they planned,
getting quite drunk.
She's not beautiful,
quite plainly dressed,
in overalls,
in her early 50s. But the men
look up and drink,
admiring her no-makeup,
her aloofness,
joking to see her smile blandly
and glide away,
making empty plates vanish
like any hope of her number.
They are in love for once
without desire, as she recites
tonight's specials
from memory, taking orders
in her head too,
forgetting nothing, leaving them all
feeling that care and
distance are what they wanted,
not love after all.

Ode to Katie's Hairy Armpits

With hipster glasses, lipstick,
and a sleeveless black dress
cinched with a green belt
she obviously cares how she looks,
but is walking the fine line between
feeling sexy and pleasing men,
of which I know little,
especially of her, a feminist in Nebraska
who works at a woman's shelter and seems
to know everyone in this bar.

We take in the black growth
and underbrush of them, where
we're used to smooth lunar absence,
even in 2016, curly and darker
than her head: untamed groves,
wildenings, deserts which have just
now long after the disaster
begun to recover, and which
sway under her sentences, oases under
the breeze of her words.

Blind Date

They have never met only chatted online,
her voice on the phone American
brash, and his British refined, yet they
have everything – pets, films –
in common. But when they meet
it turns out she is a full four inches taller,
and the waiter's moving in already
with the waters, so they're stuck,
the tablecloth like a white flag.
They go to bed together that night
as if just to prove it's a non-issue, yet in the dark
carried away by breast and arm and cock,
they discover it's a weird turn-on
like a chase by goons, or make-up sex.
So when their friends ogle, titter,
or overcompensate too polite, they feel
ashamed, doubtful, but then randy, and rush
back home where she gets on top,
and rides him 100, 200 feet taller,
and counting, like a rocket ship
blasting off, and he below her as lush as the
earth-rise when seen from the moon.

At the Airport

There's the tallest female soldier
I've ever seen – at least 6'4" –
standing erect and mute, amidst some
middle-aged, gray or balding men,
a few customers ahead of me in line.
She's like some convex mirror
in which we're perfected:
our maleness, that burning seed,
that tender flower, in her
tough and tall.
As if to be fulfilled as men
we would have to each become a woman
who never had it easy,
with a scar on her lip,
whose life seems her own choice
as she waits to board our
plane to the latest war.

Gym Guy

Who doesn't like feeling strong
and ornamental at the gym, or get some
joy out of narcissism once and again,

which is mostly hard work
when your face is given the affective
range of the Mojave desert
in springtime

though it's fun pretending to be
the lava under it,
all that 'manly pressure' bottling up
made of Morse code and gnats
and adds for soap in the paper.

Disguised as the Morton salt girl
how much one can get away with!

Though it's all infinitely sad,
the way it hardens like a plaster
sarcophagus around
King Tut's dazzling sense
of death –

and then to go about with fistbumps, snaps,
like popcorn expanding into tiny
clouds over and over instead of
just being old bones wanting out
of the body's violin case
to sing in the earth,
to dissolve slowly, played by
the innocent moles and worms.

Un-Relatable Poem

A man cobbles his life together
as best he can, skimming
these shark-abandoned waves

but must so many pastimes lead
back to head-butting the walls of the
padded self?

In the next version, you'll play a videogame
where you'll play yourself playing yourself

And I hate how touching, we stop feeling the other
person's hand so soon, our bodies assuming
there's nothing there unless it's new

The way a man shoves another dorito into his craw

Or a priest rips another black note from his
reptilian brain and slips it into the church's
suggestion box.

Once I too prayed to god, projected
my best self upwards and spread
it in the finest mirror-net over the nightsky,
looking back down on myself in bed.

Sometimes I still confuse women with goddesses,
or a dead sea-horse floating upside down
with the treble clef of my own happiness

But sometimes I better myself
by noticing things around me:

Look. Tonight's ambulance spreads dancing jewels.

And across the park, circling the fountain,
two skateboarders have found rich
girlfriends and are balancing them in the air.

The Car Accident *(Cleves, Ohio – 7th of July)*

At the road-side next to the badger-mess
the sinking sun is coming right through
the leaves of the tree. He says the word

to himself aloud – *tree* – listening to boys still
lighting off fireworks, gazing blankly
at the far powerplant's rising clouds –

it is summer near the river, everything
is green, the tractor is wound up
in leaves, sprouting white flowers at its rusting tips.

Today, everyone's heading to the lake, to bust
their way past security and wade
right in, still holding their beers.

Not him. He has just walked five miles to
place a plastic lily and a tinsel windmill
at this goddamn cross, white and

wooden and staked by the roadside because,
fifteen years ago there, for a second, someone
was careless.

Cars rush past him honking.
An eighteen wheeler slacks off dirt.
Finished, no destination in mind, he puts out

his thumb, knowing nobody would feel safe to stop
with that white zippery scar
sliding all the way down the side

of his skull and, after waiting a minute, hikes on
toward the distant McDonalds arches,
tiny and held high as a steeple,

dark wind tugging at his sleeves.
Sun has almost set. Somewhere, another old barn's
letting light in a thousand places into its body.

Obama's Oval Office

I stood at the Oval Office's open entrance
and stared in at that cozy room, half-window
lit by blazing roses, tulips outside
against the paper-gray sky, thinking of the
man who is not here today, the great ghost
in DC's machine, how he calls himself
"the bear" at times wandering out from
his vast one-animal zoo, past snipers
on the White House roof and the guards nervous
& glad to see him, and out to the streets
for a simple lunch – everywhere the people
surprised, alert, with the wild celebrity of his
sighting, the one living statue amidst all the
giant marbled dead ones. I stood there
at his place of work while he was not there
admiring his décor, the bust of MLK
opposite his desk, the bowl of fresh apples
on the coffee table, the two Hopper paintings
of farmhouses, as if to say
the country is large and not an oval,
as the beaming black secret service agent
joked saying I had to leave, then smiled,
telling me of arrows and olives and how
he 'gets to see the man each day.'
I stood at the roped-off entrance feeling love
for the President, and a dim ache that
he would be leaving soon, who used such a
pleasant office, and did all his work there,

not in a closet hidden nearby as was rumored,
and looking in at his desk I thought
I would like to work there too it looked
so light and wholesome in the April
cloudy-sun, but I only smiled at the guard,
and leaned my neck into that room
as far as it would go, wishing for it to
grow even longer on the stem of my neck,
and breathed in deeply through my nose and
mouth, like a teenager who places to his lips
a girl's discarded sweater, and since you're
not allowed to take pictures wrote this poem.

Baying at the Moon

My Robot

My robot comes to me in the night afraid of death. I tell him he is
a young robot he will not die for a long time. I pick off the magnets
that stick to his chin, oil him, tickle music out of his chest with a
tin spoon as he laughs in even intervals of two seconds. Each night
I hear him up watching Spanish soaps, he never sleeps, volume
turned low out of kindness.

My robot lives only a year. The humidity rusts him apart. In death,
he is tiny. I place him in a shoebox and bury him in the backyard
beneath his favorite orange tree. I spear the TV antenna into
the earth over his grave. A ripe orange wobbles and falls. Its fast
Spanish breaks on a kiss.

My Failed Poems

So into the maze of the meatlocker comes this poem and cannot husband it. For none there, hornless, scalloped adrift will ring out from their scooped conchs, let alone spring back to life amidst the bluebells, their gossipy spittoons. And the part where bodies clunk down the mailshoots of Television while onions are peeled away to terror's blue crystals is a set-up already auctioned away. So into the albino palace comes this new poem ok, right up to the throne, but mumbles awkwardly, eyes glued to the wall-paper whose roses curve like the mouths of shrimp-Lincolns. Drawn on there is also a funhouse where one more poem arrives and has a decent time with all those mirrors, but can't remember it later in the poverty lines awaiting its appointed harmonica. Into the disaster the final poem cannot go but stands at its edge sipping tar and blinking at the dismayed faces of electrical outlets, pulling leaches from its arms to red welts which it tells others are love bites, it is such a sexy poem, and then up and away into the various heavens where it doesn't make it past the heaven of insects, the one where a stag-beetle humps an infinite rotting banana as the stars turn.

A Walk on the Beach

On the beach the shark is dead:
its marble eyes leak jelly, its underbelly,
slashed, bleeds pinkly onto the sand
and flies like copters circle round
reporting on the immense good fortune
of its disaster. Dead as a doornail,
whatever those are; while teenagers
sitting on top of the lighthouse
hock loogies, its fat gray tongue
sticks out a bit from the side, where
sand is stuck to it like a fillet dipped
in flour: another catch of the day,
though bigger than the horseshoe
crab's bone-shell or ripped pelican;
yes its death takes pride of place on the
beach this evening, staring
back into the waves (who turned
it that way?) as two joggers stand
back a few cautious feet taking pics,
and the tide creeps near and withdraws
not knowing what to say.

Anti-Acknowledgments

This poem was written in spite of my
uncle Denny who sliced part of my ear once and farted
drunkenly wielding the tomato knife
whose juices slid across the countertop in their
messy, viscous, delicate archipelagoes of seeds,
and left me uninspired for years.
I would like to unthank the federal government
and national culture for its cheap vocabulary
of the flesh. The lights of the city for deafening
the stars. It's true I learned a thing or two about
disappointment and to negotiate the labyrinth
of false expectations, yet really I would have
gotten this elsewhere and at a lower price.
I'd like to unthank several teachers
who think poetry is a fancy game to make them
feel fancy about themselves, and who sit
in lecture halls smirking, a chronically sour
expression like there is a tiny little homunculus
of themselves perched on their lips. This poem
is definitely written in spite of the republican party,
and yet the liberal tone of NPR makes me
comatose as a slurpee as they monologue each morning
through the lists of the numberless dead.
This poem is written in spite of you, Coach Smithy
with your watery eyes quoting us
Rudyard Kipling "the strength of the wolf
is the pack" as basketball shoes squelched and
echoed along the glistening gym floors
and one flung the ball like one's own vomited up

ego stone to stroke the patchy wisdom-beard of the net.
Written in spite of several thankless hours
of meaningless conversation with a businessman
from Tulsa who wouldn't shut up
and let me read or stop telling me his salary
on the flight from Denver. If poems are little
grapes one tries to grow inside one's head,
he smooshed a few of them, and lit a few of them
like firecrackers pulverized into a void of never-
attempted existence leaving me
numb as novocain. Does one grow to love
one's hatreds? To love or hate one's hands?
Perhaps, but not the numbing, not the laughter
at the peglegged man on the street. I'd like to unthank
the apes who kept me up last night and left me this
splitting headache through which I peer
like an undersea vessel looking for squirmy squids.
And I'd like to unthank panda bears for needing
to eat and sleep 23 hours a day and rolling over
on their young crushing them to death
and proving to me nature's idiocy and to
distrust the inviolability of love.

You are dead, Lewis Carroll

You are dead, Lewis Carroll, the young man said
And yet your hands are so strong
You are juggling two chairs, a saw, and your head
How do you get on?

In my life, chuckled sadly the poet
I shook when I tucked in a sheet
I screamed when I walked in a field of roses
And couldn't make out my feet.

You are dead, said the boy, beg your pardon,
But you cure modern diseases
And you twist-tie stars to posts in your garden
Where they float and shine in the breezes.

Well in my life, the photographer said
From the crack in the tree there came voices
Which said one life's as good as another
So don't make any choices.

You are dead, said the boy, please excuse me
But you pop grapes into wines
And sleep high up in a spiral tree
Smiling and dressed to the nines.

You are right, the corpse said, I indulge
Far too much for my age
But when I grew up in the Battle of the Bulge
I played the Marseillaise on my cage.

You are so dead, said the baby, please tell me
How to live a real life
Should I work hard at learning to spell
Should I think of taking a wife?

Oh to be living, smiled the kind homme,
You'll figure it out I guess.
Now leave me it's time for my lesson in drums
And you make me a little depressed.

Ivy League Graduation Speech

Though you graduated from here,
you have only dragged things out:
eventually you will be spared nothing.
After so much has been
done for you, you will know what it is
to be a means for others' ends, your time
a commodity, your life something to sell.
They've told you to believe in yourself,
to take chances, dream big – but
these are uninspired lies useful to
keep your energy up, which is not
nothing, but amoral as caffeine.
Know, though, there are small moments in
which you can choose over and over
again your life: restraining yourself
from saying something knee-jerk,
speaking up in a silent meeting about
an obvious but unpopular reform.
Now come forth and shake our hands
firmly, pose for a few snapshots, then
make room for those who are next,
a long, endless line waiting behind you.

Theme Park

America tangle with me, hybrid with me
and what bored surveillance footage,
stored in decades of black and white?

The roar is a wound.
Top 40 songs grow from it. Grow through
each finned speaker like a bad crop.

Someone taps me on the shoulder,
mistaking. Was I the good lover,
given over to the motions of goodness?

Screams: a blur of upside faces.
O from the cramp that many people
in a line is at last we are here

at last, America, climbing shaken
the wooden ties, up to where sweat makes
Rorschachs of the girl in front's shirt

and desire does horrible things to our body
pushed and held back into the seat.
Plastered there as we summit.

Look: the skytower, the parking lot's rows
of palms and chrome. We fall for
minutes into loveliness. And into the

downward sky, endless. Just a shade
of yellow on my brain where America
is nervously pressing its finger.

The New Me

The moon is the best tombstone
I know, the least horrible one
and the sun wants to
burn everything down,

so it's only for the great
frigid distances of space
that we survive at all.

Underneath the letters of each stop sign
you find an inscrutable
diamond-image that bleats and
tells you it's too late.

What sad songs lurk in the vacuumed carpet.
What silky math tricked you
into that binary dead-alive.

But do you ever have that day when
you rise up in a strange room,
and all the threads hooked into you
vanish, a sail without a boat
lifting up in a rustling like
pigeons off an old man's body?

When a man sets his own house
on fire with a lighter and breath freshener
he's not trying to speed up time,
he's trying to molt.

So too when I'm barefoot spraying
windex into the dark of amplifiers
or menacing birds by flapping
my ugly stick-arms,

I'm trying to brandish a new me
like a toy pistol straight from
the factory, ripped from the packaging.

Bang! says the little white flag.
You're somebody else.

In the Fields

The Hair

When he finds out his wife has cancer
they go together to the barbers and get their heads
shaved sitting in chairs side by side.
The barbers are shocked and don't think of cancer
because their hair is beautiful, and both the same kind
of Nordic blond, long, like movie stars.
Putting their hairs into baggies
into her purse, they go on to the mall
to get tattoos that say *bring it on*,
and all of their friends think it's romantic.
But her death is still bad, dozens of trips in
and out of the emergency room, nursing homes,
hours writhing in the bed-hell,
unable to follow what's on television, while
he stares into her body like it's the sea.

After the funeral he looks at them, and realizes
he doesn't know which bag of hair is hers and
which is his. On a whim, pours them together into
a larger bag and sleeps on it
like a pillow that first night until, waking to a pulsing
throb in his neck, switches over to a real one.
The very next day, goes out and donates them
to Locks of Love where they are sewn together
into a beautiful blond wig, where another
woman, whose failing marriage and job
as a bank cashier has made all her hair
fall out, picks it up. Her husband loves it,
and they make love for the first time in a year,
and he pulls and draws down socks, skirt,
blouse, bra, panties, one by one, delicately

until he reaches up and she lets him
take off last the wig – her baldness gleaming
a little in the lamplight, their cries pitched over the
San Francisco apartment windows drowned
by the hipsters whooping on their way
from bar to bar, and a train far off.
Each time they take the wig off last before getting
into bed together, her bald head suddenly sexy
like a Platonic ideal.

One day, driving up
the coast, they pull over by the seaside
to take a picture and the wind takes it right
off her head, flinging it over the waves, waving
like a gloved hand, goodbye, like a white seagull,
and they make love almost immediately,
recklessly in the car, her fingers in his mouth,
his fingers cradling her smooth, smooth head.
And the day after, he goes out and buys her
another wig, long and blond and as close
to the first one as he can find, and keeps buying her
new blond ones for holidays, birthdays, so,
though her hair never really grows back, though
she's never promoted, things improve, he
can really see her – almost all the time – love her,
and they have three good years before
he's jackknifed on the freeway on the way to work,
drunk driver, his body split nearly in half.

After that, she becomes obsessed, buys herself
many more wigs, blond and long, fills her big

closet-cubbies with them, how an heiress stores
shoes, ringlets refracting in the closet's tall mirrors.

A year later
she runs into the first husband at a bar
who has let his own long hair grow back, all
ringleted and blond, and she loves it right away,
strikes up a conversation where
he tells her about his dead wife *who had hair
just like her wig*. But she isn't really listening
entranced by his own hair, touching it,
letting him buy her drinks, pulling him
into a cab giddy, he, slightly guilty because
she looks so much like his wife. At her home
as they undress and begin to embrace, she
stops, saying she needs to confess something and,
taking him by the hand, opens the closet of wigs
where he sees his wife's blond hair
multiplied by a hundred, then by thousands in
the tall mirrors. Then sees, as though for
the first time, this stranger-woman, multiplied
too to the horizons, standing naked and bald
at the very center of her own grief and beauty.

No other world

6AM: on a road in Indiana
rests the stag-head, slightly off-middle,
just missing the white hyphens.

The antlers rise from the head like
handholds or something dripped in a cave.
The sky is the cadmium blue of an empty
cement swimming pool.
No skidmarks, no body.

The head has been there for three days:
many quick glances from
cars, swervings, towards and away.

Now, the man in the orange jacket
steps up and spears it, drawing over it gently,
the eyelid of his large black bag.

Now, the man cocks his head, listening
to a rustling in the summer fields.

Walmart Poem *(Lawrenceburg, Indiana)*

Among the aisles,
not looking now, I sense the cameras over me
like Chagall's beautiful strangers.

The women drift by in their little car-machines.

Wah wah, says the fat man
to himself standing among a thousand
unlit, scented candles.

Some children flee a furious echoing.

And then through the black veil
into the chill of the freezer section
to become for a second the old man there
who pauses to select one
from a thousand packets of meat.

Williamsburg, Kentucky

On a gray day, the green mountains surround us:
like a demented Johnny Appleseed,
poked and itchy, I trot after the stranger,
hugging the black trash bag to my chest, bloated
with extra straw poking out through its sides.
Done with the reseeding of Otis's grave, we have straw
to spare for a balding insurance salesman, who,
as I spoon out handfuls, keeps making prayer hands at me
until the flecks fall and clump into a kind
of blanket or police outline over his sister.
The grave beside it's still bare though: plowed by rain,
it has sunken in now to form a muddy, greenish
pool where earthworms curl into the four O's
of my helpless phrase, *sorry for your loss*.

Love Poem for Lindsay in an Iowa Tornado Ten Years Ago

Since the woman I love, before I ever met her,
has only a locked closet and a walkman,
she blots out, as best she can, the siren's
terrible keening with Whitney Houston's
pre-drug-ravaged voice – the one Oprah
once called a "national treasure" –
and as the twister skips right down her street,
she avoids coats and brooms, kicks her limbs
up, shuffles her shoulders in a dance
so private I can't stop imagining it.

Leap Day Birthday

Today, a bright one in February,
sun made it down almost the whole way
into the courtyard. Knucklebones of tiny trees.
Arc of shadow on brick and glass
as something enormous comes near, and
decides to withdraw, peering out of the
vertiginous blue, as it does sometimes.
No, the off-years are better,
the feeling something's special, different, but the clue *only*
no worry that it means anything,
that it will be solved, going from prologue
to epilogue all at once, a better marker this
absence, this instant of midnight which ingests
a day's vanishing, this invisible hummingbird,
which alights on my life for an instant and is gone.

Every Dog Has His Day

My girlfriend and best friend's dogs are both
dead this winter one after another
one in Boston where it's the snowiest winter in history
one in Nebraska where it's just Nebraska
both friends thinner somehow their dog sidekicks removed
both friends plainer, more exposed and lovelier
like the bone under the skin,
the wolf-cry in their throats gone,
and gone the running back and forth over the meadows
the helter-skelter movement of their walk
the half imaginary friend they would talk to by their feet
is now fully imaginary, and I am not a substitute
as 1500 miles from each other they take themselves on walks
as they reach out into the air and pull their hands back
as they ponder the coldness of architecture
as they square off with winter
how fearful and bereft I am seeing them a little
bit gone into this loss, and what a fierce vision it is:
two ones I love and two urns to be scattered.

I Have Lots of Hearts

I have lots of hearts, it's grisly.
I leave them bloody, soaking the pillow.
I keep them in a drawer where they turn gray.

It's a bother having so many.
Some are stretched as waterskins, snakeskins.
Some glitter like precious stones, are as cold.

But my hearts are non-biodegradable:
they are made of kevlar and teflon.
They glow in the dark, but don't light my way.
They whisper bad advice to me like bridesmaids,

telling me to gift each one away.
'Take this, it's all of me,' I lie, already a new heart
growing inside me like a dark pearl
or shadow of a disease on an ultrasound.

My Other Grandparents

Drink Me, says his death.
Keep Your Head Down,
says her death. Known now through
stress-lines engraved on the brows
of three living daughters all just
over five foot tall and thirty years later.

My living grandparents trace
lineage back to Romania, shtetl,
Palestine, Abraham.

My other grandparents like a lopped limb,
a clearing, a nuptial flush of June
grasses, where they hold each other,
bells ringing, listening to the sound
like a gunshot a long way off.

Birthday Poem

Thank you, life, for the 23,000 breaths
I took yesterday, for the 206 bones
of my body, not a single one broken.
Thanks for my 13 major organs all healthy,
for a vision whose blur is correctable,
for ears only a little deaf thus far.
Thanks for my mysterious sturdy formation,
how cars, pens, books, shirts, roses all wear out
but my body repairs itself.
But thanks above all for my gondolier heart,
which when I awoke last night,
anxious and fearful, kept beating,
pushing the blood back,
drawing me toward dawn.

And now, the real acknowledgments:

A huge thank you to the editors of the following publications, in which many of the poems from this book first appeared:

American Poetry Review, *Antioch Review*, *Baltimore Review*, *Café Review*, *Chattahoochee Review*, *Cincinnati Review*, *Conjunctions*, *Connotation Press*, *Cortland Review*, *Crab Creek Review*, *DMQ Review*, *Hanging Loose*, *Harpur Palate*, *Harvard Advocate*, *Hotel Amerika*, *Lake Effect*, *Literary Review*, *Massachusetts Review*, *National Poetry Review*, *Natural Bridge*, *New Delta Review*, *North American Review*, *One*, *Rattle*, *Rhino Poetry*, *River Styx*, *Salamander*, *Sewanee Review*, *Southern Poetry Review*, *Southwest Review*, *Spillway*, *Tampa Review*, *Vallum*, *Water~Stone Review*, *Willow Springs*, and *Zyzzyva*.

"Woman and Dogs" was reprinted in *The Practice of Creative Writing* Third Edition (Macmillan); "Contemporaries" was the winner of the 2014 *River Styx* International Poetry Contest; "Americas" was a runner-up for *Rhino Poetry's* Founders' Prize, and a nominee for the Pushcart Prize; "Theme Park" was the winner of *Harvard Advocate's* Contest Issue.

Thank you to my parents Kathryn and Samuel, my brother Gabe, my aunt Laurie, and my grandmother Rosalind.

I am grateful to a number of poets and teachers who helped with these poems directly or indirectly: Jorie Graham, Peter Sacks, Lisa New, Stephen Burt, Philip Fisher, Eric Idsvoog, Mark Levine, and Dean Young.

And to friends without whom these poems could not have been written: Mande Zecca, Emily Adams, Gabriel Houck, Jay Deshpande, Tom Roberts, Jim Pautz, Jessica Lucey, Christopher Le Coney, Charlie Maule, Rebecca Graff, Brenden Millstein, Dan, Miki, and Dave Donoho, Peter, Deborah, Sarah, and Leo Goldberg, Martin Reames and Darlene Mitchell.

Thank you to Richard Krawiec and to the lovely people at Jacar Press.

And to Lindsay, true partner.

Adam Scheffler grew up in California, received his MFA in poetry from the Iowa Writers' Workshop, and is currently finishing his PhD in English at Harvard.